LEICESTER MURDER STORIES

RECALLING THE EVENTS OF SOME OF LEICESTERSHIRE'S
MOST WELL KNOWN MURDERS

David J A Bell

BRADWELL
BOOKS

Published by Bradwell Books

9 Orgreave Close Sheffield S13 9NP

Email: books@bradwellbooks.co.uk

British Library Cataloguing in Publication Data: a catalogue
record for this book is available from the British Library.

1st Edition

ISBN: 9781909914292

Print: Gomer Press, Llandysul, Ceredigion SA44 4JL

Design by: Andrew Caffrey
Typesetting by: Mark Titterton

Photograph Credits: Photography by the Author
unless otherwise stated

CONTENTS

INTRODUCTION

In this book of Leicestershire murders, the fifteen stories range from 1760 to 1986. In 1760, the aristocratic Earl Ferrers took his usual practice of being violent to his servants one stage further. He shot and killed John Johnson, a perfectly innocent man who had served both the earl and his father. When he was tried for his crime by the House of Lords, Earl Ferrers became the last peer of the realm to be hanged.

Following the murder of a girl in 1986, the investigation made international headlines by being the first ever use of DNA fingerprinting (itself discovered at Leicester University) to find the killer.

Also included is a case where three young Coalville miners were found guilty of murdering a pedlar. When, on the scaffold, one of them confessed that he alone had committed the crime, the authorities still hanged all three. Add in the case of a man who tried to conceal his crime by burning the body of his victim, a local wrestler who drowned his wife in a mill race, plus the infamous Green Bicycle murder of 1919, and the reader will find much of interest in the crimes that have occurred in the county of Leicestershire.

David J A Bell

THE ARISTOCRATIC MURDERER

IN 1745, LAURENCE SHIRLEY INHERITED HIS TITLE – EARL FERRERS – AT THE AGE OF 25. HE HAD ATTENDED OXFORD UNIVERSITY, BUT LEFT WITHOUT TAKING A DEGREE. HE OWNED ESTATES SPREAD OVER THREE COUNTIES BUT LIVED AT STAUNTON HAROLD IN LEICESTERSHIRE. HE WAS SAID TO BE AN ECCENTRIC, BUT THIS WAS A EUPHEMISM FOR BEING A BAD-TEMPERED, ARROGANT AND VIOLENT MAN. HE INSISTED ON HAVING HIS OWN WAY IN ALL MATTERS, LARGE OR SMALL. HE HATED BEING CROSSED BY ANYONE.

His insane rages were not helped by his prodigious appetite for alcohol. He was disliked by many of his fellow peers, and had been excommunicated from the Church of England. This must have embarrassed his younger brother, the Revd Walter Shirley. His bouts of bad temper were notorious. On one occasion, when

Staunton Harold, the former home of Earl Ferrers

guests failed to turn up to dine with him, he took a horsewhip and beat a number of his servants. On another, he went to collect a horse that was being looked after by a Peter Williams. Because the earl was unsatisfied with its condition, he knocked down Mrs Williams and ran Peter Williams through the shoulder with a sword.

He did have other interests besides drinking and being violent. He had an eye for pretty girls, and took a mistress called Margaret Clifford, the daughter of his agent. She bore him four daughters in five years, but, being illegitimate and female, they had no claim on his estate. His family was urging him to marry and produce some legitimate – preferably male – heirs. However, for some reason none of the local aristocrats wanted their daughters to marry Earl Ferrers. He had to go as far as Cheshire before he found a girl prepared to marry him. She was Mary Meredith, the pretty young daughter of Sir William Meredith of Henbury. She was 16, half the age of her bridegroom.

It will come as no surprise that he treated Mary badly. One small indication of this is that, before getting into bed with her, he always put a loaded pistol by his side, telling his wife that he might shoot her before morning! Because of this and his continuous violence, Mary was granted a legal separation from the Earl by Act of Parliament, and was also awarded money to be paid to her annually. In the 1750s, this form of divorce and alimony was quite rare, and it is an indication of the extent of Earl Ferrers' brutal reputation.

The trustees needed to appoint a man to collect the rents of some of the farms and have the money paid to the ex-Lady Ferrers. Not surprisingly, nobody wanted the job. They knew it would mean trouble. The earl instructed John Johnson, a man who had been a faithful servant to both him and his father, to take the position, saying that Johnson was the only man he trusted. Johnson was reluctant, but when the earl insisted his will was obeyed.

It wasn't long before Earl Ferrers had changed his attitude, saying that Johnson was trying to cheat him. He tried to have Johnson evicted from his cottage at Lount, but the trustees intervened on his behalf. This incensed the earl, and he even made the ludicrous accusation that the sober and upright Johnson might be having an affair with his ex-wife. He told Mistress Clifford that the man needed shooting.

On Sunday 13th January 1760, Earl Ferrers called at Johnson's house. He was apparently in a friendly mood, and even gave Johnson's children some foreign coins. He then instructed John Johnson to come to see him at three o'clock on the following Friday.

On that day, before Johnson arrived, Earl Ferrers sent away all the male servants, plus his mistress and the four daughters. The only servants left were three maidservants: Elizabeth Doleman, Elizabeth Saxon and Elizabeth Burgoland. I suspect that the earl couldn't cope with servants with different names and called all his female servants Elizabeth.

When Johnson arrived, Earl Ferrers kept him waiting outside for ten minutes then admitted him into his study. The maids heard the earl shouting, followed by the sound of a shot. Ferrers came out and said to Elizabeth Doleman that she should go in and attend to Johnson 'as he's been shot'. The injured man was taken to lie on a bed, but the unrepentant aristocrat came in and seized the man's head, telling him, 'I should have put the bullet through your head instead of your body.'

Dr Kirkland, from Ashby-de-la-Zouch, was sent for. When the doctor heard what had happened he took the precaution of calling at Lount Pit and borrowing six burly coalminers. When they arrived at Staunton Harold, the earl was clearly inebriated and waving a gun about, threatening to shoot anyone who tried to arrest him. He was eventually persuaded to let the doctor in. When he examined Johnson, Dr Kirkland could see that he was fatally wounded, but he had the sense to tell the earl that the victim would soon recover.

The doctor remained at Staunton Harold for the rest of the day. He had to listen to the ramblings of the drunken aristocrat, complaining of all the neighbours he hated, and boasting of all the conquests of local girls he'd achieved. He insisted that the wounded Johnson was not to be taken away from Staunton Harold, but once he'd fallen into a drunken sleep the doctor had Johnson loaded into a chaise and carried back to his home at Lount.

When Johnson died at 9am the next day, Dr Kirkland was faced with a dilemma. A murder had been committed, it was clear who was responsible, but the murderer was Earl Ferrers, the local nobleman who was a power in the area. Nevertheless, the doctor went back to Staunton Harold – again with a posse of coalminers – and the earl was arrested. He was lodged at the White Hart in Ashby while an inquest was held. A verdict of 'wilful murder' was brought in, and the earl was taken first to Leicester county gaol and then to the Tower of London.

A man can only be tried by his peers, and this was quite literally the case in this instance, as the only court that could try Earl Ferrers was the House of Lords. In his two months in the Tower, Ferrers cut down on his drinking. All he consumed was a pint of brandy with his breakfast, a pint of wine with his dinner and a pint of wine with his supper. Virtually teetotal by his standards.

At his trail, Ferrers decided to conduct his own defence. Dr Kirkland gave his evidence, and the three Elizabeths, who had never been more than a mile from Staunton Harold before, went to London to say what they had seen and heard. At the suggestion of his family, the earl decided to plead insanity. Various witnesses gave evidence, but when Peter Williams described how the earl had stabbed him when he collected the horse, the judge intervened to say, 'Good God, man, that's not insane. If the man was negligent in his care of your horse, any one of us would have done the same.'

The earl argued his case clearly and cogently, but this proved his undoing. The Lords decided that if he spoke with 'wit and sagacity' he must be sane. He was found guilty and sentenced to death by hanging. The eccentric earl then petitioned to be beheaded, as hanging was for commoners, but this plea was ignored.

On the scaffold at Tyburn (now Marble Arch), the earl insisted on being hanged in his white and silver wedding suit, since it was his wedding, he claimed, that had brought him to this place. He then said that if he hadn't been drunk at his engagement and in the days before his wedding, he would never have married in the first place.

There was an undignified fracas on the scaffold, when the earl gave a £5 tip to the assistant hangman. It was common for a wealthy man about to be hanged to tip the hangman, who would send a man under the stage to hang on the condemned man's feet to speed the death. On this occasion, there was a public punch-up between the hangman and his assistant over the £5. I think the money must have eventually gone to the right man, because the earl took only four minutes to die.

His body was cut open, put on display for four days, then buried in St Pancras Church. Twenty-two years later it was disinterred and brought back to Leicestershire, and it was placed in the family vault at Staunton Harold church.

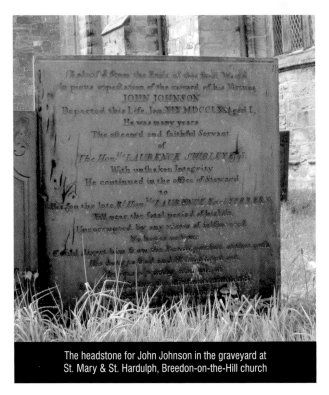

The headstone for John Johnson in the graveyard at
St. Mary & St. Hardulph, Breedon-on-the-Hill church

John Johnson was buried more humbly in the churchyard
of Breedon-on-the-Hill. On his grave, it states that
Johnson was 'a faithful servant to two Earl Ferrers.'
There is no mention of the fact that one of them killed
him! Some have historians have claimed, however, that
the fact that a nobleman was hanged for shooting a
servant prevented England from having a French-style
revolution, and getting rid of all the aristocrats.

THE JEALOUS HUSBAND

JOHN WILLIAM NEWELL – ALWAYS KNOWN AS WILLIAM – LIVED WITH HIS WIFE ISABELLA AND THEIR SIX CHILDREN IN WOODGATE, LOUGHBOROUGH, WHERE HIS WIFE RAN A GROCERY SHOP. HE HAD SPENT 22 YEARS IN THE ROYAL MARINES, RISING TO THE RANK OF COLOUR SERGEANT, BUT HAD RETURNED TO CIVILIAN LIFE AS A CARETAKER OF A LOCAL HALL. HE ALSO HAD A PENSION FROM HIS SERVICE CAREER. WILLIAM AND ISABELLA SEEMED A HAPPY AND SETTLED COUPLE UNTIL HE BECAME OBSESSED WITH A NOTION THAT ISABELLA WAS HAVING A RELATIONSHIP WITH A FRIEND, HERBERT HOARES. HE WAS MAD WITH JEALOUSY, EVEN HIDING ROUND CORNERS TO SPY ON HIS OWN HOUSE, TO SEE IF HERBERT WOULD CALL ON ISABELLA. THERE SEEMS TO HAVE BEEN NOTHING TO HAVE ROUSED HIS SUSPICION. TO EVERYONE WHO KNEW THEM, ISABELLA WAS CLEARLY A GOOD WIFE AND MOTHER, WITH NO INTEREST AT ALL IN HAVING AN AFFAIR.

Nevertheless, William was convinced of her adultery and he began to drink excessively. When drunk, he would turn on Isabella, abusing her verbally and physically.

He even threatened to kill her, which caused him to be bound over by magistrates to keep the peace. He found it impossible to obey this order, and one Tuesday morning in August 1894 the couple had a terrible row, which led to violence. The two older children, Blanche and Lucy, left for work at 6.30am, but after that the row between William and Isabella escalated. Billy, who was only eight, woke to see his father attacking his mother with a coal hammer. William struck Isabella over the head several times with the weapon, causing significant injuries, then left the house and opened a bottle of whisky.

Billy and three other children ran from the house in a panic and raised the alarm. PC Hall arrived on the scene at 7am, to find a gory sight. The walls and floor were splashed with blood. Isabella Newell was still alive when the policeman got there, but by 9am she had succumbed to her injuries and was dead. The guilty husband, who was still drinking whisky in a neighbour's garden, was soon arrested and charged with murder. After he was arrested, he declared: 'I'll go to the gallows in good heart if I know she is dead.'

He tried to claim that the murder was an unpremeditated act committed during a moment of temporary madness, but two doctors both pronounced him sane. His eldest daughter, sixteen-year-old Blanche, gave evidence that William was not drunk on the evening before the attack. She added that she had seen her father hit her mother on many occasions, even after he had been bound over to keep the peace.

Her evidence was to prove vital in the trial held in November. William Newell was found guilty and sentenced to death. Petitions for a reprieve were organised both locally and in Plymouth and Chatham, where Newell had been based during his life as a Marine, but the home secretary, Herbert Asquith, turned down all pleas for mercy, saying that they were groundless.

In prison, William Newell was described as a well-behaved prisoner. He put his affairs in order, arranging to pay off all his debts and setting in progress the adoption of his soon-to be-orphaned children. Newell was hanged by James Billington in Leicester Prison at 8am on 10th December 1894 at the age of 42. Two press representatives were allowed to witness his execution, although this was the last time this happened in Leicester.

'THE GENTLE GIANT'

WHEN A MAN KILLS TWICE IN LESS THAN TWO YEARS, AND HIS VICTIMS HAVE NO CONNECTION TO ONE ANOTHER, THEN IT IS NOT UNREASONABLE TO SEE HIM AS A POTENTIAL SERIAL KILLER. IF HE IS CAUGHT AFTER THE SECOND MURDER, THEN THE POLICE HAVE ALMOST CERTAINLY PREVENTED THE KILLING OF FUTURE VICTIMS.

Paul Bostock is one such killer. He was six feet five inches tall and weighed 15 stones, but was described as a 'gentle giant'. His former headmaster described him as a nice boy, conscientious and popular. His karate instructor said that 'He was polite and placid, and never lost his temper.' His rugby coach stated that Paul disliked aggression and violence, grumbling that it was 'very difficult to get some fire into his belly'. And yet within this gentle giant lay a much darker aspect to his personality: an obsession with acts of violence and killing.

When he was sixteen he committed his first murder. His victim on that occasion was Caroline Osborne, a 33-year-old with her own business, an animal-grooming parlour called Clippapet. She was amicably separated from her husband Gary. She had no steady boyfriend but enjoyed a full social life. She loved her work, and her future seemed bright.

On the evening of Friday 29th July 1983, she took two dogs – her own black Labrador and a neighbour's retriever – for a walk on Aylestone Meadows, an area lying between the Grand Union Canal section of the River Soar and the River Biam. Unfortunately for Caroline, she had left her other dog, a fiercely protective German Shepherd, at home. Later that night the black Labrador returned home alone. Neighbours heard the dog howling and called the police.

The towpath at Aylestone Meadows

The initial search of the towpath and undergrowth along the River Soar proved unfruitful, but at 10.30 the next morning, PC David Warsop was out with his police dog. The dog led his handler down an embankment where Caroline's body was lying in some long grass. The first problem was the presence of the retriever, which had remained with the body all night, and which would not allow anyone to approach. The retriever's owner was brought to the spot and her dog came to her immediately. The police could now examine the body. Caroline was fully clothed but her feet and ankles were tied together. She had been stabbed to death.

An animal behaviourist, Dr Roger Mugford, said that the retriever and Labrador had acted as a co-operative and intelligent team. He said that it was not unusual for there to be an understanding between them – that one dog should stay with its owner and the other should go for help.

The police murder squad investigating the killing was led by Detective Superintendant Alan Stagg. Swabs were taken from the two dogs, and an inch-by-inch search of the undergrowth was undertaken, while frogmen searched the river. House-to-house enquiries were made in the streets to the west and north of Aylestone Meadows. The locality housed both a sports ground and a nature sanctuary, and it was an area popular with courting couples. Alan Stagg called on anyone who was on Aylestone Meadows on the Friday evening to come forward, particularly if they had seen the auburn-haired Caroline Osborne, or a black dog wandering loose. He also warned that the killer could strike again, and advised that women and girls should not go out into lonely spots on their own.

The inquest revealed that Caroline had been stabbed ten times in the neck, chest and arms, and that her ankles had been bound after her death. The police enquiries continued, but despite being featured on Crimewatch a year later, the investigation got nowhere. Paul Bostock had got away with murder.

On Saturday 27th April 1985, at 4pm, a young nurse was stabbed to death on Chantry Lane, a footpath near Groby Road hospital. Amanda Weedon was 21, and she had spent her lunchtime shopping with her fiancé. The couple were about to collect the keys to their new house. Amanda had set off from a friend's house at Beaumont Leys at 3.45, and was walking along the footpath to the hospital. The body was found at 4.15pm, and a doctor from the hospital tried unsuccessfully to revive the injured girl. She had been stabbed seventeen times in the neck, chest and thigh. Her handbag had been taken. It had contained only a small amount of cash and a bankcard, though the bankcard was found later in the nearby Gilroes Cemetery.

Chantry Lane

A witness came forward, and the police announced that they were looking for a tall man in dark clothing, probably khaki or olive green, who had been seen on the footpath at 4.05, close to the murder spot. Olive Weir from Beaumont Leys thought that the description sounded like her grandson, Paul, who used her garage as a fitness studio. She strongly advised him to go to the police and clear his name. Eventually, he did so.

From the moment Paul – Paul Bostock – walked into the police station, the solution of the two murders drew closer. While he was being questioned, police officers went and searched his home on Blakesly Walk. What they found there convinced them that they had the killer. On the wall were posters of ritual killings and tortures. They found a collection of knives and martial arts weapons. Then they found his 1984 diary. On the page for 28th/29th July, exactly twelve months after the Caroline Osborne murder, they found the handwritten words 'Anniversary 1 year'.

At his trial in June1986, Paul Bostock was described as a sadist with an unhealthy fascination for knives and the occult. It was said that he had tied Caroline Osborne's hands and feet before goading and stabbing her. Two years later, after visiting Caroline's grave in Gilroes Cemetery, he had killed Amanda Weedon on the footpath near the hospital where she worked. On this occasion he had disposed of the knife in the cemetery, near the murder scene, but had been seen there by witnesses.

On being found guilty, he was sentenced by the judge, Mr Justice Tucker, to life imprisonment for the murder of Amanda Weedon, and to be detained during Her Majesty's Pleasure for the earlier murder. After the trial one of the detectives on the case stated that if Paul Bostock had still on the loose, they would have been looking for another Yorkshire Ripper.

TOPSY TURVEY

JOHN MASSEY WAS A LEICESTERSHIRE HEDGER AND DITCHER FROM THE VILLAGE OF BILSTONE, NEAR TWYCROSS. HE WAS A TOUGH, THICKSET MAN WITH NO REAL FRIENDS, JUST A FEW HARD-DRINKING CRONIES. HE WAS NOTORIOUS FOR HIS BAD TEMPER AND VIOLENT BEHAVIOUR, ESPECIALLY WHEN DRUNK. HIS FIRST WIFE HAD DIED – PROBABLY THROUGH A MIXTURE OF NEGLECT AND ILL-TREATMENT – AND HE'D MARRIED A WIDOW WITH A YOUNG DAUGHTER.

He was famous in the locality under his other name: Topsy Turvey. He was a wrestler, and he got his unusual nickname from his claim that he could throw any man from four counties over his head. The four counties were Leicestershire, Staffordshire, Derbyshire and Warwickshire – Bilstone is only five miles from No Man's Heath, where the four counties meet.

In 1801, Topsy Turvey was on his way home from the pub when he met his new wife and stepdaughter. We do not know what his wife said to him. Perhaps it was

'Your dinner's in the bin,' or 'Look at the state of you!' Whatever she said, it drove the man into a fury. He beat up his wife so badly that she suffered a broken leg. He then picked up the injured woman and carried her to Bilstone watermill, where he threw her into the mill race. Unable to stay afloat, the injured woman sank and was drowned.

Bilstone Water Mill, where John Massey threw in his wife

The poor woman's ten-year-old daughter tried to intervene but the brutal wrestler threw her into the mill race too. However, she swam to the side and survived. She gave evidence at the trial of John Massey when he was charged with the murder of his wife. The trial was held in Leicester, where the judge was Baron Vaughan.

The man was found guilty, and sentenced to death. At this stage, he made a somewhat crass request, saying that he knew he was going to die, but would they please bury him between his two wives! A strange request, considering he had murdered at least one of them. He didn't get his way. He was hanged at Red Hill, and then his dead body was taken back to Bilstone where he'd committed the crime. It was put in iron bands and then suspended from a gibbet.

There was a difference between a scaffold and a gibbet: you died on a scaffold but you were already dead when you were hung on a gibbet. The common practice of gibbeting the body of a hanged man was intended to act as a warning to anyone else who might be thinking of behaving in the same manner. I'm not sure how much of a deterrent it was though, as his old drinking companions used to walk home with an extra pint of beer, and pour it into Topsy Turvey's mouth.

It might be assumed that most bodies were gibbeted for a week or two to frighten the locals, but in the case of John Massey that assumption would be way out. His body hung on the Bilstone gibbet for an incredible eighteen years, long after the flesh had rotted from his bones!

John Massey was not the last man to be gibbeted in Leicestershire. That dubious honour belongs to James

Cook, who was hanged and gibbeted in Leicester in 1832, though his body was taken down after a few days. However, it seems likely that Massey holds the record for the longest time for a man to be suspended from a gibbet.

The gibbet post at Bilstone

The very gibbet post from which John Massey was suspended can still be seen on the lane from Twycross to Bilstone, called – not surprisingly – Gibbet Road. It has a low fence round it, and a noticeboard giving the details of the evil murder committed by Topsy Turvey. At one time there was a smaller notice about the crime actually attached to the gibbet post, but this kept being stolen by souvenir hunters and vandals.

Even in the early 19th century, there were such souvenir hunters. In 1818, someone stole Topsy Turvey's skull. It was taken across the county border into Atherstone, Warwickshire, where it was turned into a drinking tankard. It is widely believed to be still kept in the safe of a pub in the back streets of the town. Although I have not been able to verify the story, I have been told by several local people that once a year it is brought out and sits proudly on the bar, after the traditional Atherstone Shrove Tuesday football game.

THE KLA EXECUTION

RED HILL FARM, NEAR THE VILLAGE OF SAPCOTE, BELONGED TO BROTHERS ARTHUR AND ROY TALLIS. ROY LIVED IN HINCKLEY BUT ARTHUR AND HIS WIFE JOYCE LIVED IN THE FARMHOUSE. ON THE EVENING OF SUNDAY 5TH SEPTEMBER 1984, ARTHUR AND JOYCE WERE DRIVING HOME AFTER VISITING FRIENDS IN STONEY STANTON. THEY TURNED INTO THEIR DRIVEWAY AND HAD DRIVEN ABOUT 40 YARDS WHEN THE CAR HEADLIGHTS PICKED UP AN OBJECT LYING ON THE GROUND. IT LOOKED LIKE A PILE OF RAGS, BUT WHEN ARTHUR STOPPED THE CAR AND WALKED OVER TO IT, HE COULD SEE IT WAS A BODY, WITH BLOOD AROUND THE FACE. HE GOT BACK IN THE CAR AND DROVE STRAIGHT TO HINCKLEY POLICE STATION.

When the police came to the farm, they found that the body was that of a man dressed in a black coat and hat, a grey suit and a white shirt. There was a cloth tied around his head. The home office pathologist found that the man had been shot in the head and body at point-blank range. Forensic investigation established that the

The drive at Red Hill Farm, where the body was found

shooting had taken place on the spot. The body was soon identified as an Indian diplomat. He was 48-year-old Ravindra Mhatre, the Assistant High Commissioner based at the Indian High Commission in Birmingham. He had been last seen on the Friday, being bundled into a car near his home. His kidnapping had been followed by a ransom demand sent to Reuters News Agency from the previously unknown Kashmir Liberation Army (KLA), demanding the release of several Kashmiri prisoners held in Indian gaols, plus a million pounds.

Kashmir is one of the most beautiful places in the world, a high valley with forests and lakes surrounded by snow-capped mountains. The Mughal emperors had described it as paradise. Located in the Himalayan mountains, it shares borders with Pakistan and China. When India was partitioned in 1947, the Maharaja of Kashmir, a Hindu, opted to become independent rather than join the new Pakistan, despite the fact that three-quarters of Kashmiris were Muslim. Pakistan has always claimed Kashmir as its own province.

The people of Kashmir are split three ways on the issue, some wishing Kashmir to be part of Pakistan, others preferring to remain part of India, and a substantial group wanting to achieve an independent Kashmir. The politics of the area are complex and continually changing, with small radical groups splitting off from more orthodox bodies. It was thought that the KLA might have been a breakaway group from the long-established Kashmir Liberation Front, though the KLF denied any knowledge of the KLA.

Although Ravindra Mhatre had been based in Birmingham, his work had covered the whole of the Midlands and he was well known in Leicester. Ratilal Ganatra, president of the Federation of Indian Organisations, said, 'The social harmony and good race relations of Leicester must not be harmed by this terrible act. People should react calmly.' On 26th February, a memorial service for the murdered man was held at Belgrave Neighbourhood centre, and in typical Leicester fashion, it was attended by Sikhs, Hindus, Muslims and Jains. Brain Pollard, the Assistant Chief Constable, described the diplomat as a gentle, quiet family man who had spent his life in the service of others. Councillor Yusef Chaudery commented, 'I am pleased to see that, in spite of what has happened, we have maintained our unity. That unity will bring whoever has committed this brutal murder to justice.'

By the end of February, four men had been arrested in connection with the kidnapping and unlawful imprisonment of Ravindra Mhatre. By May this had risen to five, and two of the five had also been charged with the murder. All five were members of the KLF. The two charged with the killing of the diplomat were 22-year-old Mohammed Riaz, a student at Leicester Polytechnic, and 27-year-old Abdul Raja, a student from Paris. A sixth man, who was not a member of the KLF, was charged with attempting to obtain a false passport for Raja.

The trial of the six men began on 14th January 1985. Six days into the trial all the accused men changed their pleas. One admitted the kidnap, and he and two others pleaded guilty to concealing and disposing of evidence. A sixth man admitted to making a false statement to obtain a passport. All four were remanded in custody to await sentencing.

Shortly after this, Riaz and Raja admitted holding the diplomat at a secret address, but both men continued to plead not guilty to his murder. Raja stated that when he agreed to take part in the operation, he had no idea that Mr Mhatre was going to be killed. He claimed that he was horrified when the man was shot in front of him. Riaz, of Jarrom Street, Leicester, said that he had never intended that the diplomat should be shot. He claimed that he had been driven from Leicester to Birmingham by Mushrat Iqbal, a member of the KLA, who had told him that he would have to guard Mr Mhatre while negotiations were taking place for the release of political prisoners being held in Kashmir. Riaz continued his evidence, saying that two days after the kidnapping, he travelled in the car that took the diplomat to Sapcote, along with three other men. Riaz claimed that he remained in the car while the other men got out with Mr Mhatre. He turned the car round and picked up the other men, who were 'shaken and panicky'. They told him that they had shot the kidnapped man.

The trial lasted for 16 days. The jury found Riaz and Raja guilty of murder and both were sentenced to life imprisonment. A third man received a 29-year sentence for kidnapping and concealing evidence while knowing a murder had been committed. Two others who had admitted helping the offenders were given two and three-year sentences. A sixth man was fined £500 for making a false statement to obtain a passport. Attempts by the Home Secretary Leon Brittan to have Iqbal and two other men extradited from Pakistan were unsuccessful.

BURNING THE EVIDENCE

JAMES COOK WAS A LEICESTER BOOKBINDER, WITH A HOME IN WHEAT STREET AND A WORKSHOP IN WELLINGTON STREET. IN 1832, HE WAS BEING PRESSED FOR PAYMENT OF A DEBT OF TWELVE SHILLINGS (60P) BY A LONDON ENGRAVER AND TOOL CUTTER NAMED JOHN PAAS. BECAUSE COOK SEEMED TO HAVE NO INTENTION OF PAYING, JOHN PAAS TRAVELLED UP TO LEICESTER TO COLLECT THE MONEY IN PERSON. WHEN HE ARRIVED AT THE WELLINGTON STREET PREMISES, JAMES COOK DECIDED TO CANCEL THE DEBT BY BEATING HIS VISITOR TO DEATH WITH AN IRON BAR.

He now had the problem of getting rid of the body. After fortifying himself with alcohol, he then set about the gruesome task of dismembering his victim with a meat cleaver and a saw. After further liquid fortification, he decided he would now burn the evidence. After lighting a fire in his open grate, the 21-year-old bookbinder began to incinerate the pieces of the dead man. It was a time-consuming occupation and took him most of the day. He was drinking continuously as he did it, and ended the day in a very intoxicated state. After throwing the last piece of the dead man's body onto the blazing fire, he locked up the workshop, and began an unsteady stagger back to his Wheat Street home, where he fell asleep.

However, during the night, the chimney of the Wellington Street premises caught fire, and neighbours had to break in. They found a large piece of 'meat' blazing away in the fireplace, and fetched James Cook from his home. He tried to explain the situation by saying that he'd bought some meat for his dog but had found it to be rotten and decided to burn it. The neighbours thought this a bit suspicious, but did allow the bookbinder to lock up again and go home.

Once home, Cook realised the game was up and he left Leicester. He walked the ten miles to Loughborough, where he boarded a stagecoach heading for Manchester. He then headed for Liverpool, where he hoped to find a ship.

The next day, surgeons examined the meat from the fire in the Wellington Street workshop and found it to be a human thigh bone and pelvis. In the Wellington Street workshop, the police found a leather pencil case and bloodstained clothing belonging to James Paas. A warrant for Cook's arrest was issued, and a reward was put up for his capture. Two local policemen set out in pursuit, and caught up with him as he was being rowed out from the dockside to a ship bound for America. He had almost made it. Cook jumped off the rowing boat and tried to swim ashore, but was soon taken prisoner and brought back to Leicester to stand trial.

He admitted his guilt, making a full confession, so his trial was a mere formality. The judge, Baron Vaughan, sentenced him to death. Two days later, he was hanged outside Welford Road gaol in front of a cheering crowd of 30,000 spectators.

A public hanging was an occasion of great interest and a ghoulish form of entertainment. Men would take their whole family to watch, along with food and drink, and even telescopes to get a better view of the dying man. It was meant to be a deterrent to others, but the fact is that, despite the fact that thieves could be sentenced to death, a public execution, with its huge crowds, was the best day of the year for the local pickpockets.

After the hanging, James Cook's dead body was put on display. It was suspended from a gibbet at the junction of Aylestone Road and Saffron Lane, and a further 20,000 people came to look at it. The people who came to gawk at the grisly sight were so badly behaved – they were described as 'riotous and licentious'– that the authorities took down the corpse and buried it on the spot. The practice of the public gibbeting of the corpses of hanged criminals was soon abandoned in Leicestershire.

The original gibbet irons used on James Cook were on display at Leicester Guildhall for many years, but in December 1944 they were moved to the National Police Museum near Rugby, and a replica set is now displayed at the Guildhall, which is situated next to Leicester Cathedral.

THE COLIN PITCHFORK MURDERS

COLIN PITCHFORK, LIKE PAUL BOSTOCK, WAS A SERIAL KILLER IN THE MAKING WHO WAS FORTUNATELY STOPPED BY BEING CAUGHT AFTER HIS SECOND MURDER. THE WAY IN WHICH HE WAS CAUGHT MAKES THE CASE ONE OF THE MOST IMPORTANT IN INTERNATIONAL CRIMINAL HISTORY.

In November 1983, he had murdered 15-year-old Lynda Mann on a footpath known locally as the Black Pad, in the village of Narborough. Lynda had walked to the neighbouring village of Enderby to visit a friend. As she walked back at 7.30pm, a man was waiting on the Black Pad. It was Colin Pitchfork, and he was about to attack and strangle her. Pitchfork's wife was at an evening class, and had left him minding their son. While Pitchfork was committing the murder, the young boy was strapped into a baby seat in his car, parked just along the road.

The Black Pad footpath, where Lynda Mann was murdered

Although Lynda's family reported her missing, the police didn't take it very seriously at first. They thought that she was either out with a boyfriend or with a gang of mates, and she had forgotten the time. Her stepfather knew her better than they did, and went out that night on an unsuccessful attempt to search for her. Her body was found at 7.20am the next day by a man on his way to work at the nearby hospital, Carlton Hayes.

The first thing the police did was to take Lynda's stepdad, Eddie Eastwood, in for questioning. The grounds seem to have been that he wasn't her biological father, he had grown up on a large Leicester council estate, and he had changed his name to Eastwood by deed poll (he was a keen Clint fan). Luckily, he had spent the evening playing darts with an off-duty policeman. Despite a team of 150 police officers working on the case, the enquiry fizzled out, and a year later there were only two officers still on it.

Meanwhile, at Leicester University, a research scientist named Alec Jeffreys had discovered a process that would become known as DNA fingerprinting. Every individual has chromosomes which carry DNA, unique to that individual. The authorities were quick to realise that it would be possible to check any traces of blood, sweat or other body fluids found at the scene of a crime with the DNA of a suspect. Alec was awarded a full professorship at the university, and was later knighted for his work.

Colin Pitchfork struck again on Thursday 31st July 1986, and this time it was in daylight. Dawn Ashworth, again a girl of 15, had walked from her home in Enderby to visit a friend in Narborough. It was four o'clock and a July evening, so she decided that, instead of using the road, she would go via Ten Pound Lane – also known as Green Lane – a grassy track with a hay field on one side and farmland bordering Carlton Hays Hospital on the other.

Dawn reached Narborough safely, but found that her friend had gone out. Retracing her route home she once again walked along Ten Pound Lane. As with Lynda Mann, three years earlier, a solitary man – Colin Pitchfork – stood and watched her.

Dawn's friend rang her home at five o'clock to say that she was sorry that she'd been out when Dawn called at her house. Dawn's father simply said that Dawn hadn't got back yet. When she still hadn't returned by 9.30pm, he rang the police. This time the police took the disappearance seriously. Dawn was the same age as Lynda, and had disappeared in the same area. A massive police search began. Dawn's body was found in bushes by Ten Pound Lane, covered with branches and nettles. Like Lynda Mann, she had been violated and strangled.

The police became very interested in a young man on a motorbike, who had been seen riding it along Ten Pound Lane a day earlier. A female police officer recalled that a youth in a red motorcycle helmet had been taking a lot of interest in the search for the missing girl. They also found out that he had described to a friend the precise location where Dawn's body had been found before that information had been officially disclosed.

It was not belong before the young man – a 19-year-old porter from the hospital – had been found and taken in for questioning. Determined to get a confession, the police interviewed him at Wigston police station for 15 hours. Eventually, he confessed to the murder of Dawn Ashworth, then denied it, then admitted it once again. However, he refused to admit that he had murdered Lynda Mann, three years earlier.

The police were certain that the two murders must have been committed by the same killer, and sent samples from the two dead girls and from the man who'd confessed to the second murder to Alec Jeffreys at Leicester University. His findings were astonishing. Yes, both murders were by the same killer – but it wasn't the youth in custody. He had to be released.

The police were back to square one. They had two murders, three years apart, and no real suspects. On 1st January 1987 an unprecedented decision was made. All male residents of Narborough, Littlethorpe and Enderby who had been aged between 14 and 31 at the time of the 1983 murder would be 'invited' to give a blood and saliva sample, along with all patients from Carlton Hays Hospital and any male with any connection to the area who had no alibi for the two murder dates. The numbers involved were enormous. The Daily Mail headline for 2nd January read: 'Murder Test for 2000 Men'. Participation was voluntary but the community pressure was such that anyone invited went along.

Dramatic twist in double killer hunt

MURDER TEST FOR 2000 MEN

The police decide to DNA test all local men

In his home in Littlethorpe, Colin Pitchfork had a problem. His invitation had come, but he dare not give the required sample. He resolved the problem by involving a workmate from the Hampshire Bakery named Ian Kelly. He told Ian that he had taken the place of a friend who was frightened of needles, and had given a blood sample in his place. Now that he'd received his own invitation, he needed someone to do the same for him, so that the police didn't have two identical samples of DNA. Somehow he managed to get Ian to swallow this preposterous story. They doctored Colin's passport by pasting In Ian's photograph, and it was Ian Kelly who gave the required samples in the name of Colin Pitchfork.

Later, however, Ian mentioned what he had done to some workmates and one of them informed the police. Kelly was arrested and then Pitchfork. Colin Pitchfork admitted the crimes, and described what he had done in full detail. So keen was he to talk about the events that he insisted in starting his story again when any new policemen came into the room, so that they didn't miss any of the unpleasant details. Pitchfork was later diagnosed as a psychopath. He possessed some superficial charm, but was completely unable to feel empathy. He showed no signs of anxiety or distress while being questioned. Although he could utter verbal statements of regret, these had no meaning for him.

Colin Pitchfork was tried in Leicester in January 1988, found guilty, and received two life sentences for the murders and two ten year sentences for the assaults. He also received a three-year sentence for the conspiracy with Ian Kelly. Kelly was perhaps fortunate to receive just a suspended eighteen-month sentence for his actions. Even the judge may have felt he was being lenient, as he added, 'I just about believe you did it because you accepted the story put forward by Pitchfork.'

For the first time in history, DNA fingerprinting had been used to solve a murder case, although with Colin Pitchfork it was a fear of the process, rather than the science, that had led to his capture. If Ian Kelly had not gossiped about it, and if a female colleague had not been public spirited enough to repeat that gossip to the police, the truth might never have come out.

PEPPERMINT BILLY

WILLIAM BROWN WAS BORN IN THE VILLAGE OF SCALFORD, ABOUT FOUR MILES NORTH OF MELTON MOWBRAY. HE HAD TWO NICKNAMES, BLINKING BILLY AND PEPPERMINT BILLY. HE GOT THE FORMER FROM AN EYE AFFLICTION THAT MADE HIM BLINK CONTINUOUSLY. NOT SURPRISINGLY HE DID NOT LIKE BEING CALLED BY THIS ONE. HIS OTHER NICKNAME CAME FROM HIS FATHER'S OCCUPATION AS A MAKER OF PEPPERMINTS.

Billy got into bad company and in 1843, when he was 20, he was found guilty of stealing some silver spoons in Newtown Linford. He was sentenced to ten years' transportation. When the authorities wanted a punishment that was worse than imprisonment but short of execution, the guilty person would be sent to the other side of the world, often to Australia, to serve his sentence there. In Peppermint Billy's case, he was transported to Tasmania.

The majority of men who were transported served their sentence, and then settled down there. They married – there were women prisoners transported too – and lived the rest of their lives as farmers. However, in 1856, three years after his ten-year sentence had ended Peppermint Billy came back to England.

In October a baker named Alfred Routen set out in the early morning from his home in Asfordby on his way to Grantham. After passing through Melton, he came to the toll gate at Thorpe Arnold. He called out, but the gatekeeper – 70-year-old Edward Woodcock – did not appear. Alfred went into the gatehouse and found the body of the gatekeeper lying on the floor, alongside the body of his 10-year-old grandson, James. Edward Woodcock had been stabbed and shot in the chest, while the boy's throat had been cut.

The police were sent for, and the man who took charge of the case was Frederick Goodyear, the Chief Constable of Leicestershire. Back then, the Chief Constable was a hands-on working police officer. There was a significant item left on the premises. It was a large pistol – as used by Australian bushrangers.

Two witnesses came forward. Joe Burbridge described a man who had asked him whether Woodcock lived alone at the gatehouse. A boy named Henry Read said that two days earlier a man had grumbled that the gatekeeper had refused him a drink of water. Both Henry and Joe described the same man, saying that he was tall and thin, and that he blinked all the time. They were both describing Blinking Billy. And his home in Scalford was only few miles from the gatehouse.

A reward for the capture of William Brown was offered and his description was circulated all over the country. Four days later, a publican in Weatherby was reading this description of the wanted man when a stranger walked into his pub. The stranger was tall, thin and he couldn't stop blinking. The man was apprehended and brought back to Melton by train. He appeared before the magistrates, and was remanded in custody until his trial at the next assizes. Peppermint Billy denied being the murderer, but when his bloodstained clothes, found near the Thorpe Arnold gatehouse, were produced, his guilt was proved. And his fate was sealed.

His motive for the killings was never discovered. It could have been revenge. On the ship coming back from Australia, he had been heard swearing he would kill those who had brought about his transportation. It is just possible that Edward Woodcock had given evidence at his original trial for stealing the silver spoons. However, it is more likely that he was intending to rob the gatehouse, and killed the gatekeeper in the process. Young James Woodcock died simply because he was staying with his grandfather.

Peppermint Billy was hanged outside the gates of Welford Road prison before a crowd of 25,000 spectators, at Leicestershire's last public hanging. On the scaffold he behaved with some dignity. He did not cry out or weep, or claim a recent conversion to religion. People in Scalford must have been incredibly laid back, because his father, who had just seen his son hanged, came out with the phlegmatic comment, 'Well done, Billy. Yer've died a brick.'

THE SQUADRON LEADER

The Grand Hotel in Leicester, where Josef and Joan had met to talk about their future

TAXI DRIVER FRANK TIMSON PICKED UP TWO PASSENGERS FROM THE GRAND HOTEL IN LEICESTER AT 2PM ON SATURDAY 24TH JANUARY 1948, AND WAS TOLD TO TAKE THEM TO 200 KITCHENER ROAD. BEFORE THEY GOT THERE, THE MALE PASSENGER GAVE HIM A £1 NOTE AND TOLD HIM IT WOULD COVER THE FARE PLUS A TIP. FRANK WAS DELIGHTED, BECAUSE HE'D BEEN GIVEN A TIP THAT WAS FOUR TIMES AS MUCH AS THE FOUR-SHILLING FARE. HE WAS LESS THAN DELIGHTED WHEN HE TURNED ROUND AND SAW THAT THE MAN HAD TAKEN OUT A PISTOL AND WAS POINTING IT AT THE WOMAN WHO WAS WITH HIM. THE MAN THEN GAVE FRANK ANOTHER £7, AND TOLD HIM, 'WHEN WE GET THERE, FETCH THE POLICE.'

When Frank pulled up at the Kitchener Street address, the woman began to get up, saying, 'I don't care. I'm not frightened.' The man then shot her four or five times at point-blank range before turning the gun on himself. He pointed the gun at his temple and fired twice. The woman fell from the taxi, landing on the pavement. The man slumped back on the back seat of the taxi.

Frank ran into the house and told a lodger to call the police and an ambulance. When he went back outside, the body of the woman was still lying on the pavement, but the man was climbing out of the car with the pistol in his hand. He handed the astonished driver three letters, and said, 'I have shot her five times and tried to kill myself twice.' He then tried to reload his gun, a Mauser automatic, and said that he would try to shoot himself again.

At this stage, two police officers, Inspector Harold Toach and Sergeant Bill Joiner, arrived on the scene. Inspector Toach disarmed the man before he could kill himself. The man – Squadron Leader Josef Zawadski – was cautioned. He took the three letters from the taxi driver and handed them to the police. One of the letters was addressed to his commanding officer, one to the police and the third to Kathryn Henson, the mother of the woman he'd just shot.

Zawadski was taken to Leicester Royal Infirmary, where he received treatment to his head wounds, which were not serious. When he came round, he could not remember the events that had led him there until he was shown a newspaper account of what he had done. He stated that he was glad that Joan Henson was dead, adding, 'It was a murder of the heart.' He later stated, 'I am ready to die. I want to be shot like a Polish gentleman, not hanged.'

The police began to put together the tragic story of Josef Zawadski and Joan Henson. Joan had spent her childhood in Canada before coming to England with her parents. At the age of 18, she had married a paint merchant who had then been called up into the army. In 1942, Joan had met the handsome young Polish Air Force officer, and she fell in love with him. Josef Zawadski immediately told her that he had been married to a German girl, who had left him, but Joan omitted to mention her own married status. Josef and Joan became lovers, and soon set up home together. The couple appeared very happy, and Josef got on well with Joan's mother, Kathryn, who thoroughly approved of her daughter's choice of partner. Kathryn regarded Josef as a real gentleman; kind and caring, with impeccable good manners. He was generous too, giving Joan an allowance of £10 per week, an enormous sum in the early 1940s.

In May 1946, the couple had a baby son, Andrew, who rapidly became the apple of his father's eye. Even the news that Joan had been married before, which came out when her ex sued for divorce, did not seem to alter Josef's affection and respect for his beloved wife.

However, in the summer of 1947 Joan began to find her relationship with her Polish lover claustrophobic. He had very old-fashioned views, and did not approve of some of Joan's friends, commenting that they were not respectable women. To Joan, her Polish lover seemed over-controlling and dictatorial. Feeling trapped, she decided to leave Josef, and she and little Andrew moved into lodgings in Kitchener Street. She had been a stenographer and an ex-member of the ATS, but she now took up a job working in the Turkey Café in Granby Street. Josef was desperate to get his family back and begged her to return. Joan agreed to meet him on the Saturday afternoon, which raised his hopes of reconciliation. They met at the Grand Hotel, but he was distraught when she told him that she would never come back to him. They left the hotel in a taxi, but he shot her before they got to her lodgings.

At his trial for murder, the squadron leader stood to attention as he pleaded not guilty to murder on the grounds that he was not sane at the time of the killing. Two of his letters were produced in evidence. To the police, he had written tersely, 'Dear Sirs, Sorry to be trouble, but it cannot be helped. I shall kill her, Mrs Zawadski, for personal reasons. I shall kill myself. Yours faithfully . . .'

The letter to Joan's mother was longer and more emotional. He wrote, 'Darling Mummy, Terribly sorry there cannot be another way. I shall kill her and myself and finish my tortures. Please arrange something for Andrew's future. Sorry I cannot do that. Cannot live any longer. There may be some money for Andrew at my station. Try and get it. Thanks very much for everything. You were always so nice to me. Josef.'

Josef's commanding officer, Wing Commander D.A. Upton, stated that he thought Josef had been in a 'pretty bad way' lately, compared with his normal demeanour, and he was 'mentally worried and shaken'. Kathryn Henson described Josef as a devoted father, and said that he had been very generous to her daughter while they were together.

Dr Arthur Colahan, a Leicester neurologist, said that, in his opinion, Josef Zawadski was suffering from manic depressive insanity at the time of the murder, and would not have known that what he did in the taxi was wrong. He added that jealousy had not played a part in his actions. However, Dr A.B. Graying, the medical officer at Leicester prison, stated that he believed Zawadski was normal and knew what he was doing when he fired the shots. In his summing up, Mr Justice Cassels acknowledged the gallant war service of Squadron Leader Zawadski, but then launched into an impassioned speech, saying that 'shootings and the use of knives are contrary to our British natures'. The comment about knives seems irrelevant to the case, and the judge seemed to be emphasising that Josef was foreign and not British.

The jury brought in a verdict that Josef Zawadski was guilty but insane, and the judge sentenced him to be detained during His Majesty's pleasure. Kathryn Henson commented afterwards that Josef had perfect manners and a pleasing personality. 'The trouble was that he loved her too much.'

A TRIPLE HANGING

JOE TUGBY WAS A PEDLAR FROM COUNTY DURHAM, WHO CAME TO COALVILLE IN AUGUST 1877 TO SELL WARES TO THE MINERS AND THEIR WIVES. COINCIDENTALLY, THE VERY FIRST MINERS IN COALVILLE WERE ALSO FROM THE COUNTY DURHAM AREA.

Joe spent the last night of his life in the Stamford and Warrington Arms in the town's High Street. He joined in the singing with three young colliers: James Satchwell, John Upton and John Swift. The four men were chatting and joking, and from time to time Joe was teasing the three young miners about a biscuit tin he had with him. He was winding them up and refusing to let them see what was in it. The three young men were curious about its contents, as Joe seemed to be hinting it was either cash or something valuable.

When Joe left the pub, he walked up Station Street – now called Hotel Street – to the footbridge over the railway line, unaware that he was being followed by his three fellow drinkers. They caught up with him on the footbridge, and an argument began over the tin. Soon Joseph was receiving a savage beating. His biscuit tin was opened but it proved to be disappointingly empty.

The fatally wounded pedlar was found near the bridge by two other miners just after midnight, the empty biscuit tin beside him. Constable Hardy was sent for, and the wounded man was first taken back to the pub and then on to the Ashby Union, being transported there in a wheelbarrow. Constable Hardy wrote in his police notebook: 'August 31st. Found Tugby laying at the bottom of the steps of the foot railway bridge, all over bruises. Took him to the union. He died at 10am the next day.' This was a very terse and unemotional account of the death of Joseph Tugby.

The pedestrian footbridge over the railway.
The original bridge had steep metal steps.

After the fracas on the bridge, James Satchwell and John Upton had gone on to another Coalville pub, the Royal Oak. They were discussing what had happened, and were overheard by a man named Charles Clifton. He sent for the police and the two men were questioned. James made a statement that the assault had been done by 19-year-old John Swift, the absent member of the trio. He said that Swift had asked him and Upton to keep garrison – to keep watch – while he 'sorted out' Joe Tugby. When passers-by were heard, young John Swift had panicked and kicked the pedlar down the metal steps. James Satchwell and John Upton were arrested and charged with wilful murder, and a search for John Swift was begun.

On 4th September, four days later, the police received a letter from Richard Page, a wheelwright and well-known local evangelist. The letter stated that Richard believed that the missing man was hiding in his parents' cottage in Grange Road, Hugglescote. Constable Hardy went to the cottage accompanied by Inspector Brewill and Inspector Clark. They searched the premises but found no sign of the young man. Then PC Hardy spotted a trapdoor in the ceiling. A ladder was fetched, and, hiding behind some boxes in the corner of the attic, they discovered the man they were seeking.

John Swift was arrested and charged. When he heard what James Satchwell had told the police, he came out with a different version, in which Satchwell was the one who'd beaten and kicked the pedlar, then kicked him down the steps.

The trial of the three young men was held in November. The jury heard the two versions of the events, but could not decide which one was the truth. They found them all guilty, but added a recommendation for mercy. The judge was having nothing of it. He ignored the recommendation and ordered that all three should be hanged.

The hanging took place on 27th November, and it occurred inside Welford Road prison. It was the first execution to be performed inside the prison, all previous ones having taken place in public outside. Poor behaviour at public hangings had led to a decision by the authorities to conduct hangings inside the prison, away from the public. This led to the local Leicester Journal calling it 'a secret execution', and campaigning for members of the press to be allowed to attend future hangings.

On the scaffold, young John Swift made a statement saying that he had lied. He alone had attacked the pedlar, and his two friends had played no part in his death. It might have been expected that his public confession would have led to pardons for the two innocent members of the trio, but the authorities were having none of that. There had been a trial and a sentence, and they certainly didn't want the trouble of doing it all again. 'Get on with it!' was their command, and despite the fact that only one of them was guilty, all three young miners were hanged. It was Leicestershire's last triple hanging.

GUN SIEGE IN WEST KNIGHTON

LAMBOURNE ROAD IS A STREET OF SEMI-DETACHED HOUSES IN THE RESPECTABLE SUBURB OF WEST KNIGHTON IN LEICESTER. SO WHAT HAPPENED THERE IN SEPTEMBER 1975 CAME AS A COMPLETE SHOCK. IT BEGAN HARMLESSLY. IT WAS 10.30PM, AND THREE NEIGHBOURS – BETTY NIKOLOFF, WINIFRED SHENTON AND ENID CABANUIK – WERE STANDING OUTSIDE THEIR HOUSES CHATTING. A CAR PULLED UP AND A MAN GOT OUT. AFTER SHOUTING ABUSE, HE WENT TO THE BOOT OF HIS CAR AND GOT OUT A CAN OF PETROL AND A DOUBLE-BARRELLED SHOTGUN. HE RAISED THE GUN AND BEGAN TO FIRE AT THE THREE WOMEN,

---

One of the women, Enid, fell to the ground, shot dead. Winifred hid behind a wall and Betty, who had recognised the man as her ex-husband, Sabi, ran into her house and locked the door. She raced upstairs and barricaded herself in her bedroom with her ten-year-old son, Bruno. Sabi Nikoloff broke a window of the house and followed Betty up the stairs, pouring petrol behind him. Inside the bedroom, Betty opened the window, crying out for help.

The neighbours rallied round immediately. One of them, a postman, pulled the body of Enid into another drive. Three of the neighbours happened to be off-duty policemen, and one of them shouted for his wife to dial 999 and ask for the police, an ambulance and the fire brigade. With the help of others, they managed to get a ladder up to the bedroom window. Bruno and then his mother were able to descend it to safety.

However, Sabi appeared at the open window, still carrying his shotgun, and a siege began. The first to arrive was a traffic patrol car, with two police officers, followed by an ambulance crewed by Terry Wilkinson and Gerald Oakley. Next a divisional police car containing Sgt Brian 'Geordie' Dawson and PC Margaret Dayman arrived. As they assessed the situation, shots rang out from the bedroom window of 25 Lambourne Road, and Sgt Dawson fell to the ground, fatally wounded. PC Dayman also received serious wounds to her back.

With the help of local residents, the two traffic policemen decided to push the ambulance towards the house to pick up the casualties, keeping the ambulance between them and the gunman. This worked, but when Terry Wilkinson went to open the back door of his ambulance, more shots rang out. One of the off-duty policemen was wounded, but Terry was killed instantly, shot through the heart and lungs. PC Alan Dickinson made a dash to his patrol car, but as he began to send a radio message, he too was shot and wounded.

Senior police officers now appeared at the scene, including Chief Constable Alan Goodman, Assistant Chief Constable John Orme and three superintendants. Armed police officers and dog handlers were sent through the neighbouring gardens and the house was soon surrounded. A plan to fire CS gas into the house was never put into action, as Sabi Nikoloff appeared at the front window again, driven there by the fire he had lit in the house. In response to police instructions, he threw the weapon out of the window and then dropped to the ground himself. Before he could pick up the weapon again, he was seized by Alan Goodman and John Orme. He had actually been arrested by the Chief Constable and Assistant Chief Constable. It was now just before midnight, some 90 minutes after the first shots had been fired.

Floodlights were set up, and the wounded were taken to Leicester Royal Infirmary. The bodies of Mrs Cabanuik, Sgt Geordie Dawson and ambulanceman

Terry Wilkinson were examined by Dr Victor Pugh, a Home Office pathologist. Sabi Nikoloff was also taken to hospital with slight burns to his hands. In broken English, he told the police officer accompanying him, 'You are too good to help me after I done terrible things. I get my gun and I shoot her. I shoot radio in car. I burn house. I do terrible things.'

At 35 Lambourne Road, the Cabanuik family mourned the loss of a wife and mother. The ambulance service mourned the tragic death of siege hero Terry Wilkinson, a 32-year-old father of two from Braunstone, and the police force were grieving the loss of Geordie Dawson, who had served in Leicestershire for 18 years. The whole

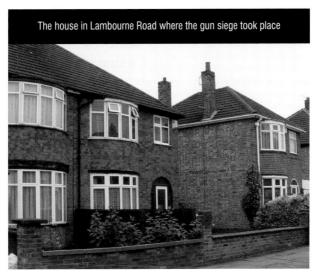

The house in Lambourne Road where the gun siege took place

of Leicester and Leicestershire shared in the grief for the senseless loss of the three lives.

The trial of Sabi Nikoloff, a 52-year-old naturalised Briton born in Bulgaria, took place in February 1976. Through an interpreter, he pleaded not guilty to the three murders, but guilty to the manslaughter of all three through diminished responsibility. The prosecution counsel said that in view of the medical evidence, he accepted those pleas. The court heard how the marriage of Sabi and Berta 'Betty' Nikoloff had been a violent one, ending in divorce. Sabi had been outraged when the divorce court ordered him to quit the house at 25 Lambourne Road, so that his wife and child could live there. He was also bitter against Enid Cabanuik, who had given evidence against him during the divorce proceedings. On the night of 1st September he had been driving along Lambourne Road and had seen his former wife and Mrs Cabanuik with another neighbour. The three women were talking and laughing, and he had been convinced that they were laughing at him, mocking him.

Enraged, he had driven to his lodgings and collected a can of petrol and his shotgun. He had returned to Lambourne Road, shot Mrs Cabanuik dead at point-blank range, and tried to shoot the other neighbour. He then pursued his wife into the house and set fire to the stairs. By the time he had broken into the front bedroom his wife and son had escaped down the ladder.

When asked about shooting at the police officers and ambulance crew, Nikoloff claimed that he was just 'shooting at shadows'. The defence counsel said that three of four doctors who had examined Nikoloff had diagnosed him as seriously mentally ill. A psychiatrist, Dr Peter Noble, told the court that the man was paranoid with delusions of persecution. Nikoloff had convinced himself that his former neighbours and the legal system were in a conspiracy against him. He said the Nikoloff's psychotic condition was worsening but was treatable, and he recommended that he should be sent to Broadmoor Secure Hospital.

However, the judge, Mr Justice May, said that while he appreciated the medical evidence, he was not sending Sabi Nikoloff to Broadmoor, but was sentencing him to gaol for life. The judge paid tribute to the courage of everyone who had helped at the siege. Seven of those who took part in the siege received either the Queen's Gallantry Medal or the George Medal, and the Queen's Commendation for brave conduct was awarded posthumously to Police Sgt Geordie Dawson and Leading Ambulanceman Terry Wilkinson. In addition, the Terry Wilkinson Trophy is awarded annually to the best ambulance student in the region.

TWO GIRLS AND A PENNYWORTH OF ARSENIC

IN 1842, STEPHEN BARNES DECIDED TO RENT A HOUSE IN OXFORD STREET, LEICESTER. THE HOUSE HAD A ROOM ON THE TOP FLOOR WHERE HE COULD INSTALL THE KNITTING FRAME WHICH PROVIDED HIS INCOME. TO SAY THE HOUSE WAS OVERCROWDED BY MODERN STANDARDS WOULD BE AN UNDERSTATEMENT. HIS OWN FAMILY WAS RELATIVELY MODEST: STEPHEN, HIS WIFE ANN, THEIR DAUGHTER MARY AND SON ISAAC. MARY WAS 18 AND ISAAC 15. WHEN THEY TOOK ON THE HOUSE, IT CAME COMPLETE WITH TWO SITTING TENANTS: MARY WARING AND SUE 'OLD SUKEY' MEE, WHO WERE BOTH ELDERLY. IT MIGHT BE CONVENIENT TO CALL MARY 'OLD MARY' TO DIFFERENTIATE BETWEEN HER AND YOUNG MARY BARNES.

Old Mary had a downstairs room to herself, and with only six people in the terraced house, there was obviously room for another. Stephen let half of Mary's room to Charlotte Barnacle, a girl just a year older than his own daughter. The modestly sized house now housed Stephen and his wife, his teenage son, two teenage girls, and two elderly female lodgers, not to mention his knitting frame in the upper storey!

The day after Charlotte moved in, she had a boyfriend come to visit her. As he stayed with Charlotte in her room until noon, Old Mary, who shared the room, wasn't very happy. After the boyfriend had left, the old lady gave Charlotte a piece of her mind, and Charlotte gave as good as she got.

The next day, the two girls, Charlotte Barnacle and Mary Barnes, went to visit a female neighbour. They talked about a recent Leicester suicide and asked innocently about poisons. The neighbour mentioned arsenic as being the most common. They were told it came in powder form, and that a very small amount would be fatal.

The two girls returned home and spent most of the afternoon in Charlotte's room. According to Isaac, Charlotte was teaching his sister the skills of binding shoes, but they were also having a very interesting conversation as they worked. In the late afternoon, they went into the city centre and tried to buy a pennyworth of arsenic from a chemist in Hotel Street. They were refused, but they had better luck in the Market Place, where the chemist, Joseph Lockyer, asked them what the arsenic was for. He was satisfied when they said it was for killing fleas and bugs, and sold it to the two young women. Laughing and joking, they returned to their home in Oxford Street. Mary went to talk to her brother, while Charlotte went into her room.

At 5pm, Old Mary came home from work on a half-hour break – although in her seventies, she was still working. Before going back to work, she filled her kettle and left it on the hearth. It was some time after this that one of the teenage girls, almost certainly Charlotte, poured the arsenic into Old Mary's kettle. Later that evening Mary Barnes went to a neighbour's house, and she bumped into an apprentice named George. Mary may have been having misgivings about the enterprise by this stage, because she confided in George that she and Charlotte had bought some 'jollop' and that Charlotte had put it in the kettle to pay Mary Waring back for some alleged offence given during a domestic dispute. When Charlotte joined them, the apprentice heard Mary say that she was worried that 'they' might taste some difference in the tea. The use of the plural 'they' rather than 'she' is interesting.

Old Mary came home from work at 9pm and joined the girls and Ann Barnes in the parlour. They heated up the water in the kettle, and Old Mary filled up her teapot with it. She went into her room to drink it. Charlotte went with her and watched as the old lady drank two cups of tea. Charlotte then went out. Fifteen minutes later Old Mary told Ann that she was feeling unwell. Soon she was suffering from stomach ache and beginning to shake. Ann Barnes poured herself a cup of tea from the same pot, but fortunately she only drank half of it. She did, however, give Old Mary another cup of tea, to 'calm her stomach'.

When Stephen Barnes came down from his work on the top floor at 11pm, he found his wife being violently sick. He decided to make her a cup of tea, and asked the girls to fill up the kettle. They went to the outside pump and added fresh water to it, but did not get rid of the poisoned water already there. He took tea to his wife, but then went down to check on Old Mary. She was now unable to speak, and she died at 2am. While he was downstairs his daughter gave him two cups of tea! Charlotte took only one sip from her cup, and young Mary refused any tea at all.

Concerned about his wife, Stephen went to fetch a doctor who lived in New Street, but was taken violently ill while he was there. The doctor – Dr John Stallard – accompanied him back to his Oxford Street home, bringing a policeman with him. Dr Stallard examined Ann Barnes and took a look at the body of Mary Waring. He then instructed the policeman to take the teapots and the kettle into safe keeping. After fetching medicine for Ann, the doctor and the policeman left, leaving the two girls the opportunity to clear up any other evidence.

Charlotte Barnacle and Mary Barnes were arrested the next day and taken to the borough police station at the Town Hall (now the Guildhall) in Town Hall Lane. Their trial for murder took place in August, before Mr Justice Patterson. Dr John Stallard gave evidence that Mary Waring had been killed by having been given a massive quantity of arsenic. His son, Dr Joseph Stallard, a hospital surgeon, testified that he had found arsenic in the water in the kettle.

In his summing up, the judge said that it would be difficult for the jury to accept that the two girls had thought that the arsenic was 'jollop' – medicine or strong liquor – because it was clear that they knew exactly what it was that they were administering to Mary Waring. He instructed the jury that this was murder, and their only duty was to decide between guilty or not guilty. The jury proved awkward, however, and insisted on bringing in a verdict of not guilty to murder, but guilty of manslaughter. Somewhat irritated, the judge said that if the young women had been found guilty of murder he would have had both of them hanged. Instead he passed a sentence of transportation. They were sent to a prison encampment in Australia for the rest of their lives.

The guilt of the two nineteen-year-old girls is not in doubt, but what was their motive? Charlotte had certainly rowed with Old Mary over a gentleman caller, but was that enough to make the girl want to kill her? Were they each egging the other on to go further and further? Was the whole thing a prank that went wrong, as the defence had claimed? Perhaps, but on the other hand the girls had enquired how much arsenic would be fatal, and had known exactly what they were buying. One other disturbing factor was that, after poisoning Mary Waring, they had given the tea made from the poisoned water to both Ann and Stephen Barnes, the parents of one of them. Their intentions remain inexplicable.

TWO SILEBY LADS

TOM PRESTON AND TOM PORTER WERE TWO LADS FROM THE VILLAGE OF SILEBY. THEY WERE BOTH SHOE WORKERS, BUT WERE KNOWN TO BE A BIT WILD. THEY LIKED A DRINK, AND WERE KNOWN TO GO IN FOR A BIT OF POACHING. THIS LED TO THEIR COMING TO THE ATTENTION OF THE TWO LOCAL BOBBIES, PC WILKINSON AND PC HALL, AND BOTH TOMS HAD CONVICTIONS FOR DRUNKENNESS AND POACHING. THE TWO YOUNG MEN – PRESTON WAS 25 AND PORTER WAS 29 – FELT THAT THE TWO POLICEMEN WERE ALWAYS PICKING ON THEM, AND A VILLAGE FEUD BEGAN. THE TWO TOMS REGARDED THEMSELVES AS GENUINE NATIVE SILEBY LADS WHEREAS THE TWO BOBBIES WERE INCOMERS FROM OTHER PARTS OF LEICESTERSHIRE (PC HALL WAS FROM SYSTON, ONLY FOUR MILES FROM SILEBY, THOUGH PC WILKINSON WAS FROM GLOOSTON, 22 MILES AWAY). THE ENMITY AND ANTAGONISM BETWEEN THE TWO POACHERS AND THE TWO BOBBIES GREW SO HEATED THAT ON ONE OCCASION TOM PRESTON HAD ISSUED A THREAT, SAYING, 'I'LL SHOOT THE PAIR OF YOU!'

On the night of Monday 25th May 1903, PC Wilkinson was on his beat in the centre of Sileby. He was walking towards King Street to meet his colleague, PC Hall, but he never got there. First he met the local butcher, Herbert Middleton, who was on his way home from the Railway Inn. The two men stopped for a friendly chat, when sounds were heard coming from the churchyard opposite. PC Wilkinson went to investigate. He shone his torch through the gate, when suddenly, two figures appeared from behind one of the gravestones and a shot was fired.

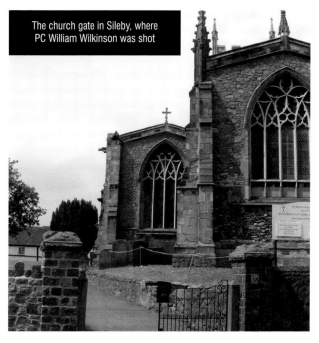

The church gate in Sileby, where PC William Wilkinson was shot

William Wilkinson had been fatally wounded with a quantity of shot that had struck him in the chest, and he died minutes later. Within an hour, police officers from Loughborough arrived in Sileby, under the command of Superintendent Agar. A murder hunt began. Given the notorious and long-standing feud, it was Tom Preston and Tom Porter who were being sought. It was known that they had been drinking in various village pubs since noon, some eleven hours before the shooting.

The police called first at an address in High Street where Preston lived with his mother and father. His concerned parents told Supt Agar that their son hadn't come home that night. The police next went to 18 Swan Street, where Tom Porter lived. They broke down the front door, only to come face to face with Porter. He was very drunk, wild-eyed and was carrying a shotgun. When he shouted that he would shoot the first man to come into his house, the police retreated. A siege began, and the police were joined by dozens of villagers who had come to watch and participate.

Both Porter and Preston appeared at an upstairs widow during the night, shouting their defiance. Many of the spectators started shouting back. At this point, Supt Agar made a strange but wily decision. He obtained some stout from the local pub and sent it in to the two besieged men. This would calm them down, and make them even more inebriated. It seemed to work, as a while later, Tom Porter was seen sitting on an upstairs windowsill smoking his pipe. At 7am the next morning, Tom Porter fired a shot into the air from the same window, then broke the gun by smashing it on the windowsill. The police arrested the pair and they were charged with the murder of PC William Adiel Wilkinson.

The trial took place a month later at Leicester Castle. The facts were plain to see, but the question as to which Tom had fired the fatal shot was never really settled. Superintendent Agar told the court that Porter had confessed to him at the time of the arrest, though Porter denied this, saying that the gun was in Preston's hands. Preston said that he thought they were just going poaching that night, and that Porter had been the one who fired the shot.

The jury, however, found them both guilty, and the death sentence was passed by the judge. They were hanged in Leicester Prison at 8am on Tuesday 21st July. The hangman and his assistant were two brothers named William and James Billington. After a breakfast of bacon and eggs, bread and butter and a pint of tea, the two prisoners had their arms pinioned behind them. They were then marched through the exercise yard to the place of execution. On the scaffold they each still proclaimed their innocence. The bolt was pulled, the two men dropped and two minutes later they were both dead.

The vicar of Sileby, who had visited Tom Preston and Tom Porter the day before their hanging, reported that they had given him a message for the other young men of the village, telling them that they should stay away from beer and all alcohol, as it was heavy drinking that had brought them to their untimely end.

WHO KILLED BELLA WRIGHT?

ONE SATURDAY EVENING IN JULY 1919, 21-YEAR-OLD BELLA WRIGHT DECIDED TO CYCLE FROM HER HOME IN STOUGHTON TO GAULBY, FIVE MILES AWAY, TO VISIT HER UNCLE GEORGE MEADOWS. ONE REASON FOR THE TRIP WAS THAT HER COUSIN MARGARET WAS DOWN FROM YORKSHIRE WITH HER HUSBAND JAMES AND THEIR NEW BABY.

Bella Wright

Bella lived with her parents in Stoughton, and she had left school at 14 to go into service, but had later found a better-paid job at Bates' Rubber Mill in Leicester. She was 'walking out' with a young lad called Archie Ward, who was away serving as a stoker in the navy. Archie's sister Sally was one of Bella's workmates.

While she was visiting, Uncle George noticed that there was a man on a green bicycle hanging about outside, and Bella explained that her bike chain had come off on the way to Gaulby, and the man on the green bike had stopped and helped her. When she left her uncle's home at 9pm, the man was still there and he and Bella cycled off together.

Her dead body was discovered 15 minutes later, lying in a pool of blood, next to her bicycle. It was on the Gartree Road, always known locally by its old name, the Via Devana. The man who found the body, a local farmer called Josiah Cowell, sent two of his farmworkers to guard it while he rode off on a horse to get help.

By 10.30, a young policeman – Alf Hall – had arrived on the scene and had taken charge of the situation. As he and the farmhands were lifting Bella's body and her bicycle onto a cart, a motor car arrived. It was Dr Kynaston Williams from Houghton-on-the-Hill. He was an opinionated man, and after doing a cursory examination of Bella's body he announced that she had died from loss of blood following a sudden haemorrhage and exhaustion from her cycling, adding that this was bound to happen if women took up cycling! The body was taken to a disused chapel in nearby Little Stretton, where Dr Williams made a second examination by candlelight, but found nothing new.

During the night, the young policeman began to have doubts about the doctor's opinion. The next morning, he went back to the Little Stretton chapel and examined the body. For the first time, he noticed, in the bruising on her face, a round hole. It looked like a bullet hole, so after reporting his findings, PC Hall went back to the spot where Bella had been found. He searched the trampled mud for some time and eventually, at 3pm, he found the bullet.

He contacted Dr Williams, and suggested that he should re-examine Bella's body. Far from appreciating the young policeman's initiative, the doctor was outraged that his medical expertise should be questioned by a young village bobby. It wasn't until PC Hall had stated that another doctor would have to be brought in that the annoyed Dr Williams agreed to come to the disused chapel and look again at Bella's body. For the first time, he took off the dead girl's hat. Not only was there a bullet wound in her face, but under her hat was a large exit wound. This implied that her hat had been put back on after she had been shot.

A police investigation began. Bella's Uncle George, a road mender with a wooden leg and a bushy beard, described the man who had left with Bella. The man was in his thirties or forties, and was well spoken. James Evans, the husband of Bella's cousin, could recall very little about the man himself, but he was able to describe his green bicycle in some detail. It was a BSA, with an unusual back-pedalling brake and a brand new gear cable. A handbill was issued by the police, describing the man and his bicycle.

The press reports about the case grew more and more sensational. One painted a picture of a scene of Bella riding her cycle and screaming for help, while the man on the green BSA pursued her with a gun in his hand. It sounded like a scene from a western, but with bikes instead of horses. A man in Leicester, reading these accounts, decided to dismantle his green bicycle. He took the pieces to the Grand Union Canal and threw them in, along with some bullets and a revolver holster. It is possible that he threw in a revolver as well.

Seven months later, in February 1920, a boatman-haulier named Enoch Whitehouse was in his barge on the canal. He was towing a second barge, and when the two vessels came close together, the tow rope sank into the water. When it came up again, there was a piece of a bicycle frame attached to it. It fell back into the water, but Enoch had noticed that it was green. He came back later with a boathook and fished it out. He then informed the police. They managed to get all of the pieces of bike out of the canal, and found the gun holster and the bullets. The revolver itself was never found.

The man who'd dismantled the bike had been crafty, and had carefully filed the bike's registration number off the crossbar. He hadn't realised that the number was repeated on the inside of the forks, and this number led the police to a shop in Derby. Their records showed that in 1910 they had sold the green BSA to a man named

Ronald Light, who was lodging in Derby at the time, but who had since moved to live with his widowed mother in Highfield Street, Leicester.

The police spoke to his mother, who told them that Ronald had moved to Cheltenham to take up a position as a Maths teacher at Dean Close School. When they spoke to the well-spoken ex-public schoolboy, in Cheltenham, he denied having met Bella Wright. Asked about the green bicycle, he initially denied owning any such bike, but later said that he couldn't be expected to remember every bike he'd ever owned. However, when both George Meadows and James Evans identified Ronald Light as the person they had seen waiting for Bella on the evening of her death, the police were sure they had the right man and he was charged with murder.

It soon emerged that Light had been educated at Stoneygate Prep school and Oakham public school. He had gained a degree in engineering, and had served in the First World War, though his military career was an unusual one. He had served for just two years as a lieutenant in the Royal Engineers, but had finished the war as a private in the artillery!

The trial of Ronald Light was held in June 1920. The prosecution was led by the Attorney General, Sir Gordon Hewitt, as the government had decided that, in order to reassure the general public, in the case of any ex-soldier

The green bicycle is carried into court (Leicestershire Constabulary)

accused of a crime involving a gun, the prosecution would be undertaken at the highest level. The defence was equally high profile. It was led by the leading defence lawyer of the time, Sir Edward Marshall Hall. It seems probable that the money to engage Marshall Hall was provided by the Freemasons, as Ronald Light's late father had been a member.

The evidence seemed overwhelming. George Meadows and James Evans identified Ronald Light as the man who had ridden off with Bella on the evening of her murder, as did a cycle shop owner who had put a new gear cable on the green BSA on the same morning. However, once the prosecution case had been made, the Attorney General disappeared back to London.

The brilliant Sir Edward Marshall Hall rose and began the defence. There was a dramatic change of tack. Light had always claimed that he was not the 'man on the green bicycle', but now admitted that he was. The new story was that he had met Bella while cycling, helped her put her bike chain back on and ridden along with her to her uncle's house. When she came out at 9pm, he had again cycled with her for a while, then they had parted and taken different routes to their respective homes in Stoughton and Leicester.

Light also admitted that the dismantled cycle found in the canal was his, as was the revolver holster and ammunition. He claimed that he had not brought back a revolver after the war. He explained that, on hearing about Bella's shooting and reading the sensational press reports about a man on a green

Ronald Light, tried for Bella Wright's murder and found not guilty

bicycle who was the main suspect, he had panicked and disposed of the cycle, the holster and the bullets. Sir Edward Marshall Hall described the gallant war service of Ronald Light – referring to him throughout the trial as Lieutenant Light, and ignoring the fact that he had been forced to resign his commission in 1916. He managed to sow enough seeds of doubt in the jury's minds, and – to the amazement of everyone in Leicestershire – they brought in a verdict of not guilty.

Ronald Light did not go back into teaching, as it was found that he had forged his testimonials to obtain his post at the school in Cheltenham. He changed his name and moved to the Isle of Sheppey in Kent. He lived there until his death in 1975, 54 years later than poor Bella Wright.

So, officially, the murder remains unsolved. Many believe that the killer had a brilliant lawyer and got away with his crime. Evidence did indeed emerge that Ronald Light had a long history of molesting women. Two girls came forward and said that he had made amorous advances to them on that very Saturday afternoon, before cycling off and finding Bella struggling with her bike chain. Although official records state that he lost his commission due to 'lack of initiative', there is evidence that the real reason was that he had in fact molested a postmistress in France. It is possible that he 'tried it on' with Bella that evening, and when she threatened to report him, he drew a revolver and shot her.

Another possibility was put forward by a writer, A.P. Mackintosh, in 1982. He postulated that she could have been shot accidentally by a farmer shooting crows. A bullet might have gone through a hedge, unknown to the farmer, and struck Bella as she cycled past. This does not explain who had put her hat back on after the shooting, in my opinion. Another possible explanation was given to me by an old lady who told me she was the daughter of Archie Ward's sister. What if Uncle Archie had come back on leave and found his sweetheart out cycling with another man. Consumed with jealousy, he could have waited until they separated, then shot the girl.

Both of these alternative scenarios seem very far-fetched to me. Of the three possibilities I have outlined, the most likely one is that Ronald Light, the man acquitted by the court, was indeed the killer. If so, it is tragic and against all natural justice that he lived a full life up to the age of 89, while his victim died before her 22nd birthday.